BIRDS
and
SQUIRRELS

By

Phillip Reese

Note

ISBN: 978-1-3999-4216-4

Hey, if you're on Amazon and you're looking for something specific, I'd really recommend searching by Fillip Reese, along with words like "art books" or "art", or, if you know it, the title of the book. It's a great way to find what you're looking for! My book BIRDS and SQUIRRELS has a little introduction that talks about why I made it. And in January 2025 I also wrote a little book called ALIENS AND ME, ART, COMMENTS, STORIES. This book is a bit different because it talks about artwork that was already in other books, but was slightly changed. It has new comments about the ideas behind the pictures. It also has some fun stories about aliens, and it's written in the same friendly style as the Brushes series, BRUSHES & MICE, MICE & BRUSHES. You can find it on Amazon's, as well as on websites where you can buy books, with the name of the marketplace in the country code. All images in the book, including the title, subtitle, text and captions, are the property of the author, so please don't reproduce any part of the book without permission. There are many other references to other publications by the author, including THE TIMES ART CAPSULE, BOLT, POEMS RIDING POEMS, BREXIT NEWS, BEFORE I LOST MY COUNTRY, etc. and soon BOLT and Jon and Bolt, and JON and Jon and Bolt, will give you a picture of the Africa and the disruptive life in which I used to live. The beautiful photographs on both covers were taken in the communal garden.

Introduction

These events took place in Harrow, HA1, north west London. If you can, use Google directions to find this location. This booklet isn't scientific, but it's very useful for all of us still ignorant of birds and squirrels.

Last summer, I bought adult tricycles and e-kits. I ended up with two spare battery holders which I cut off at the bottom.

I put them together and thought I'd make an artistic bird feeder to keep the few birds in the garden happy.

I didn't know much about birds or squirrels, but I learned what makes the feeders safe over the summer.

In the end, I made eight feeders, two of which are 'Long Johns' and the colourful one is the 'Winter Palace'.

I put one of the Long Johns up for the squirrels because they had already damaged some of the bird cages.

And this is how my adventure with birds, squirrels and cats began.

I wrote the main text in one go. I did this after my accident and I think it reflects my sense of humour.

I tried to speak my best English to the squirrels and birds. It wasn't always easy, and they told me that they found it difficult to translate too.

With so many new experiences, I think it will take some time to get the lyrics right.

The book of this long experience has been kept short, and I hope the photos are well signalled.

Thank you

Contents

Note 2

Introduction 3

BIRDS and SQUIRRELS 5

Hi Mary Ann 28

Long Johns 37

Other Observations 40

Sunshine Invites Birds 47

A summary about cage feeders 48

Zebras Also Have a Garden of Flowers 51

2025-2026 52

BIRDS and SQUIRRELS

I live in a building with thirty flats. Two of the flats are occupied by couples, and the rest are rented by single people. Most of the people who live here are between 60 and 95 years old. Imagine being independent at 95! Imagine Dona Olga, Portuguese, who is an extraordinary woman.

I'm lucky because for many years I was one of the few residents who could walk without help, but not for the last four months. I also have to watch what I eat and there are a few other rules helping to keep myself going, but I have a girlfriend who visits me regularly and she makes me the happiest man alive - a good omen for my old age.

The storm in London against old cars (and old people) caused me terrible problems because my car, while doing a thousand miles a year, was much less polluting than the big Mayor's car.

I was told I had to get rid of it. For me the car was almost new, everything was new. In the isolation where I used to live, I did not know what ULEZ was. I couldn't just scrap it, so I decided to send it to Ukraine.

I've been driving for almost 60 years. I've used it to get to my tennis club, which is in a public school in the hills above Harrow, and it's very difficult to get there by public transport.

I bought two expensive electric bikes to prepare for the inevitable change in my life. It wasn't a good idea, cycling on the local roads made me feel unsafe. I also felt shaky, off balance and scared. When it comes to driving, Harrow is not First World Britain.

Twenty years ago, there was some discipline on the roads. Now, most drivers aren't very careful and don't know about the new laws that protect cyclists and give them rights. I read them, so I can shout a lot of LOLs at the bad drivers.

I hadn't ridden a bike since I was thirteen, and, in those days, if my head was heavy, my body was very light. There were no traffic jams in Lubango, the photo is from 1964, and most of my cycling was on trails in the highest parts, about a mile up at the bottom of the visible flat head mountain.

There were no lions, leopards, buffaloes, antelopes or dangerous snakes. It was a kind of paradise, a small town surrounded by an endless expanse of virgin land with no owners and a series of flat mountains. The Mumuílas, the small local tribe, were culturally very resilient, independent and extremely peaceful. I often crossed their paths on the trails around the mountains, sometimes stopping to let them pass, sometimes they did it for me. I always felt safe, but their smell was difficult.

Uaunica futi futi, an insult I learnt from their smell, were the only words I knew from their language. Sorry, I haven't forgotten the other one, the common good morning, if I remember correctly, it's Wahlehlehpo... with 'po', as in mole, the sound prolonged a bit emphatically.

I have some good memories of the rides, but they weren't enough to convince me that electric bikes, easy as they are, were the solution to my old age woes and sudden loss of freedom.

I wasn't sure what I wanted to do. The adventure of not knowing had already cost me a lot of money. Then I read about adult tricycles on Facebook and decided to try one out. I sold an electric bike, which was the worst of the two, and started looking for a tricycle. I was running out of time as the car was about to be delivered. I had to do something.

I drove around England a few times in my little big car and bought four trikes, fixed them up, sold one, made a trailer out of another and ended up with two identical trikes.

It was a new experience for me, which was confusing and almost brought me down. I had to buy a lot of tools to repair and maintain them. I also had to store them somewhere, so I built two private sheds, one of which I use as a tool shed.

The building also has a shed where two residents can store and charge their electric scooters. I checked it and it wasn't being used properly. It had some push bikes stored on the right side and I thought, "Great! The other side will be for one of my e-trikes."

But the little two-door shed wasn't being looked after very well. It rained cats and dogs inside when the weather was bad. It was very dangerous because there were two electrical sockets, a meter, lights and other hazards, so I had to fix the shack, and I did. Now that everything is up and running, I've safely charged there my batteries dozens of times. To ensure the rules for batteries, I use a weak heater during the winter to keep the temperature in the shack at around two-three degrees Celsius.

Once the trikes were ready and roadworthy, I bought two e-kits for them. I installed them on the trikes after making some adjustments to hold the batteries, which freed up the racks.

I then had to sell the racks as I had no use for them, but no one seemed interested. The only alternative was to throw them away, but I don't have that mentality, so I had to think about what I could do with these new, beautiful, heavy, clumsy black iron tubes. I thought a lot about it and how they could be useful. It took me lots of time but:

"Eureka!"

We have a big garden and I had noticed that there weren't many small birds in it. There were lots of pigeons, but someone was

feeding them without thinking. Some people can do good, but they also feed other unwanted little guys.

I had also seen an adult squirrel that had taken up residence in the tallest tree.

Apart from the wildlife, I had also seen many cats from the neighbourhood visiting our feline hunting ground. I soon realised that they were probably tame and friendly at home, but here in the sheltered wildlife garden they were completely out of control.

Before making a bird feeder for the two battery boxes of the trikes, I wanted to find out a bit more about these new inhabitants of this very communal area.

I started with what I had seen first: our squirrel and pigeons. The pigeons make a lot of mess, I was told, so I concentrated on our local large squirrel.

The first thing I did was to use a very clean empty plastic chicken box without a lid from a shop as a feeder. I simply screwed the box to the tree and filled it with peanuts. I put another identical box in another tree for the birds, this time with seeds. I kept putting peanuts in the squirrels' feeder and noticed that a few birds from the neighbourhood were coming over to gobble them up.

"Good for them," I said: the raids were small, so no problem.

I also saw some birds in a bush in the middle of the garden picking the sunflower seeds from the other packet right in front of them.

It looked perfect, but I had not seen one of the things that pigeons and magpies love to do, which is to take over.

They didn't wait for me or my intentions. They ate all the peanuts and seeds, and with the help of the squirrel, who never misses an opportunity, they ate it all in less than twenty minutes.

Sorry, if I use 'who' for squirrels. It helps me!

My knee-jerk plan didn't work. I did not use the word 'squirrels' in the plural in vain, for I used to fill the tray as soon as I found it empty. With so much food in the garden, the big squirrel called five other squirrels, so the word 'squirrels' was correct. That is what I believed at the time and I still act on that belief, more like a behaviour, rightly or wrongly.

During the squirrels' free periods, the pigeons took over the squirrels' food tray and the magpies hijacked the small birds' tray. Things got even worse when the squirrels nicked the second tray. It was fun to watch them go from one place to another, or from one tree to another, and even to watch them fight over their pecking order.

It was fun, but...

It was clear that this was the wrong tray. I didn't want to fail, so I tried a trick. I put a one direction folding plastic lid over the trays and screwed it to the trees. It was easy for the squirrels to lift the lid and feed themselves, but I thought the pigeons and magpies would not be able to get to the trays.

The birds landed on them, the lids tilted and the big birds slid down. Soon the magpies, looking like a cross between a clown and an acrobat, found a way to get into the bowl in front of the bush in the middle of the garden. The pigeons gave up.

But the squirrels came back, or came back several times, and the food disappeared as quickly as before.

At the same time, I saw a couple of black birds building their nest in the lower bush opposite the bowl with seeds for the small birds.

Surprise, surprise, these birds never tried to eat the seeds that were for free in front of them. They would fly in and out of the garden very fast, but I couldn't tell where they were going, probably to a nearby park. The male was black but the female was dark brown. It's hard to tell from the photo, but the hidden bird seems to be one. As it is almost spring, I think we have at least one red-beaked visitor, see below if you can.

The distraction was interesting, but I was confused and my hollow marbles were working overtime. Was the type of food I had bought for them the reason for the failure? I know now that they can go off, not this case.

I didn't know. I had just searched on eBay for squirrel food, bird food and bought what I found. I hadn't read anything specific or proper about food for squirrels or birds.

All I wanted to do was separate the large birds from the small ones and keep the squirrels away. What about the squirrels? I counted five or six once, but there were probably more. I must have fed every squirrel in the area for a while. It was the same with the magpies.

I had to cut costs and the poor little birds were still at the back of the queue.

Then it occurred to me, 'The little birds need a safe feeder!

I tied the two black metal frames together, placed small pieces of cut firewood around the frame, tied them together with strong plastic ties to make a box with many entrances, and painted the sticks with bright acrylic paints (see previous page, I had paints, I'm an amateur painter).

With some food on small plastic containers stapled to a strap, I pushed in from the top and made a lid to cover this entrance. The bottom of the two shelves was almost completely free of wood. I used a piece of folded cardboard or plastic to cover it, I can't remember which.

I expected that only the small birds would be able to get through the gaps between the small pieces of wood. To conclude the job, I hung the thick, coarse bird feeder from a dry branch of the dying tree, opposite the central bush.

"Perfect! Now I can sleep."

But I was wrong, good sleep had to wait. The squirrels had made a mess of the new feeder. They had chewed through the plastic straps and cardboard or plastic, a bit confused, memory, and got in through the gaps I thought were only for the small birds.

I bought more wood and made a new layer.

This time I screwed them to the top of the remaining ones, creating more triangular shapes, or more like three-dimensional tetrahedrons, leaving wide spaces on the inside but tight on the outside.

I also used strong waterproof plastic, which builders use for many things, to cover the bottom.

It was another good dream, but frustratingly the squirrels were still getting in.

I thought, 'The gaps are still too big and the floor needs something better than a nappy.'

I bought more and more wood, well, three or four times, but the squirrels got in every time. I kept adding layers of wood on top of the ones I had already put down.

With so many layers of wood, the Winter Palace became one big polychrome 3D puzzle. I also added a large wooden lid to the bottom, which I screwed on.

I was sure the squirrels couldn't get in. The gaps were now really tiny. Until then I had to accept that the squirrels were winning:

Squirrels 8 or more - Phillip 0.

Not believing in my luck, I was waiting for them to attack and destroy everything I had done, but they didn't. They were angry and hungry, but they couldn't get through. This time I won!

I had to write down the new score:

Squirrels 8 - Phillip 1.

After a few months of tough love, I had one single point.

I called the feeder the Winter Palace. I thought the birds would be happy to have a new place to feed in plain fruitful expected harmony.

But that didn't happen: Phillip 1 for the squirrels, 0 for the birds.

I saw a couple of tits playing with it, going in and out and really enjoying a place to play, but the joy did not last long.

I have to say that the tits fight each other in a perfect, universal pecking order, just like humans in many circumstances. Nor did I know that they like to feed alone in one place… exceptions, always.

I couldn't understand what I had done wrong. All the money and work I had put in had been wasted. It was a false premise, but I had thought, 'The feeder is very big and has many different places where the little ones can be without disturbing the others.'

Then I saw a rat coming under the fence from the courtyard of the building next door. There is always a hole somewhere and the rat did not look at me or care that I was there with my camera to photograph the birds.

It crossed the garden, climbed the tree and went into the Winter Palace.

The neighbours who saw me running towards it said nothing until they saw the rat. Some even think I was feeding it. Sad!

The cage was too close to the tree. I think the birds knew about the rats, so they stopped going into the big, beautiful palace. Now that I knew the reason, I rushed to take a picture of the big rat leaving the Winter Palace.

The squirrels kept trying to break through the outer shell of the palace to get into the colourful maize, but they couldn't. Some of the weaker pieces of wood still bear the marks of their teeth, but all in vain.

After watching for a long time, I had to admit that the birds were not coming in. Was it because they were afraid? Or was it a self-made plan to please myself, my art, my ideas, my pride, instead of helping the little ones? Something had to be done. It was a difficult time for my brain.

The Winter Palace had become a beautiful, very expensive work of art. For me evidently! And it clearly was too close to the tree, making it easy for the rats to get in.

I had to think, but I had so many new things to think about, like birds and squirrels, and I didn't know much about them. It was only a matter of time, I thought. If a big rat could get into that special futuristic building, the squirrels could do the same. I had to move the cage away from the tree.

The heavy cage was suspended from a high branch of the tree by three chains: two small and heavy, and one lighter, which I used in a triangular shape to hold the vibrant sphere in two places.

The system was not flexible. The apparatus was complicated, so after closing my eyes for many minutes, my pocket money was getting feverish, I bought a lighter long chain while keeping the triangular holding shape using the old one. Then I changed the chains and moved the cage away from the trunk. I did this alone and it was very hard and dangerous.

The palace was heavy, the ground below is too steep to balance any equipment, worse on the wet grass as it was, and I had no proper supports, no ladders, nothing to help me. As always, a challenge waits for a solution.

I picked up things I found in the garden, like old barbecues, garden chairs and large plastic vases.

I piled them all up together and climbed to the top. I broke the tops of two vases, full of compost lucky me, as I lifted the heavy Winter Palace, but they stayed there, someone had had a nice chat with them, or a promise that they would soon have beautiful flowers, and so I didn't fall.

It was crazy. It wasn't as hard as my last task, which was to move the palace from the dying tree to the big one. That tree was opposite the central bush and the Council had to cut it down. The palace had to be moved to a new place on the big tree. The photo on the page 15 shows the stump of the old tree.

I was thirteen years old again, and I used all the science I remembered from school. I used my mechanical knowledge of levers, chains and other principles of mechanics. I came up with some interesting solutions that no professional would ever come up with. They would ask for the right tools, equipment, a lunch box or even a second man, one hour brake, 10 minutes work, but I had decided to take on the challenge alone.

There were other things to complete the whole thing, and many would call it a project. For example, I stopped the Winter

Palace from spinning and swinging in strong winds by anchoring a long tube (actually a couple of tubes inside other tubes) to the tree. The Winter Palace has no weight on the pole. It works by being fixed at points with contrary rotational forces parallel to the ground.

Unfortunately, I damaged the trunk of the tree with a screw that goes free inside the pipe to prevent it from moving.

I then bought and used a four-metre stick to move the chain and hold it in a locked position on the branch. This time I asked a friend to lift the Winter Palace. It took Keith a few seconds to use his back to hold the Winter Palace, which allow me then to move it to a new, safer location.

*

I was not handicapped by this crazy job. But a few months later I experienced it while doing nothing.

I was in the lounge walking, just a few metres from my place, when I fainted. I didn't remember anything, but it wasn't good. I suffered a brain injury that left me disabled, hopefully temporarily.

I am writing this page now, three months, now four, after my accident, and I still have problems walking and sleeping. I will get better, and it was this belief that made me write these words. Or the booklet.

*

It was midsummer and the Winter Palace should have been a bird feeder. But it wasn't. The squirrels were still in charge, attacking it from all sides, practising their evolutionary skills.

I was determined to win the battle against them, otherwise I would have to accept defeat. I replaced the wooden bars that the squirrels had chewed through with new ones and painted them. The squirrels broke the top of the cage, so I improved the small trap door, fitted hinges and a lock under the small bandstand to block access to the food. The bandstand was also damaged but that was my fault, I put some seeds in it and the squirrels wanted a completely free access to the bandstand and gnawed it.

I was at war with the adult squirrels. I had won my battles against the pigeons and magpies, but the squirrels were too strong. I had to try something new.

I used to watch the sky from the lounge to check the weather, and I saw a strange cylindrical object hanging from a horizontal post outside. Since I've been using a wheelchair and now a cane, I do it again almost every day, three months already, although I would prefer to go outside.

The ignored object had been there for years, never with birdseeds. True, I, we, had never thought about it. I had seen it before and thought it was just a decoration. It was rusty, but it was clear that it was a bird feeder.

The photo shows one of these things inside a protective cage with a happy safe tit. It was a useful feeder waiting for food.

I filled it with small birdseeds and hung it on a lower branch of the half-dead tree and waited.

Within minutes, the squirrels had emptied the feeder.

I went back home to think. I remembered that when I was young, we had in our garden in Africa a very big cage much taller than a giant man and larger than a few of them side by side. It had, my memory says so, two sides made of brick. One of the walls separated it from a large chicken coop.

The birdhouse had at least a dozen beautiful small birds. The black wee widow was my favourite.

Both had nets with different wires and holes, but both protected the winged occupiers from outside dangers.

But, Kwanza, my father's dog, and one of his big sons, broke into the coop once and killed seventeen chickens.

Those bandits! All because he gave away Huíla, his foxy girlfriend.

I then turned my attention back to reality and conducted an online search. I discovered that tits can fit through holes as small as one inch, but only the small ones. To my consternation, or my ignorance, there are other sizes and other birds.

I was determined to find out about the wire, the mesh, the netting and the right size of the holes.

My eBay search revealed twenty metres of chicken wire with one-inch holes at a fair price. I shaped the wire and decided on a wire cylinder around the feeder to protect it from the squirrels.

I found the perfect material to cover the top and bottom of the cylinder: plastic, a waterproof strong hard plastic that is easy to work with. I had already designed and engineered the plastic circles to cover it.

I needed to make and attach them to the top and bottom of the cylinders to start the job (the photo next page shows a cage with one of these plastic circles).

I had to finish the job.

I had the tools to cut the wire, but the cutter was bad. It left the net with dangerously sharp ends.

At first, I thought it was me, or that the wire was not the right material for the job, but I decided that the tool was the culprit

and the reason for my confusion. So, I bought a new small wire cutter which did the job perfectly.

I bought S hooks, the same shape as the ones that hold meat, but much smaller. Then I bought one a little bigger than a man's middle finger and a few smaller ones. I also bought other different hooks to connect and lock the chains. To complete the apparatus, I used some long wooden broomsticks I had at home and a bit of cable. I later bought five of these on eBay. I cut the broomsticks larger than the diameter of the cylinder I called the 'cage' and put them through the holes on either side of it.

I tightened one side of the hook and placed the S-hook firmly in the middle of the handle. This is where the feeder would be hung. Finally, I tied a small cable to the sides of the broom handle, with another S-hook in the middle of the cable.

The cage was ready to hang and this was the first of seven cages I made.

It didn't work: the squirrels went through the plastic and ate the seeds. The pigeons, surprising me, also got access to the seeds and I lost the battle again.

Was it my brain or the plastic?

Exploring the garden, I came across some large vases with plates to prevent water getting to the tiled ground.

Were these saucers? My decision was as clear and stinky as the old white and blue PH 7 purified old soap: we knew that they were not suitable for any suitable breakfast. I found some of these plates on eBay, but they were expensive, so I bought smaller ones instead (the photo shows a final squirrel-proof cage already with the best improvements).

Once again, I was wrong. The squirrels, acrobats as they are, went through the sides and it was the beginning of a thousand surprises that turned into a summer job.

I bought the bigger ones. The squirrels chewed the plastic, but it was all for nothing, it was tough for them. For the little birds, there are still lots of teeth marks there for the posterity. A lot of work for nothing, but not mine. It was the squirrels' time to lose. Good!

Another surprise was the parakeets. They had found their way around the building for the first time. Being what they are, or observant as they are, they found their way to the feeder. This happened at the end of the summer and there's a lot to discuss before we get there.

I now had a proper cage and a feeder.

I waited a few days behind the glass of a lounge window to see how the squirrels were getting on. Would they mess with the cages again?

Success! They did not get through.

The score was now:

Squirrels 11 or more, Phillip 1. The first 1 did not count.

I could see the little tits coming through the one-inch holes to hang on the feeder, get a seed and fly back to their sheltering bush nearby. However, some of the other larger birds could not get through those net perfect holes, even other tits.

"Damn! It's a never-ending story!" I thought, thinking, thinking.

No doubt it was a never-ending job to get them all what they needed without using nature's pecking order.

I had never thought about the bigger tits, so I got a new cutter and made lots of two-inch holes well above the plates. Were they too big?

I felt I was letting them down, so I googled 'British tits' and found that there are many types of them: small, large, almost no tail, big tail, different colours and so on.

It was a much more complicated picture. As usual!

I learnt that the tits that lived in or visited our garden were called coal tits and the larger ones were called great tits. I'm not sure about the colours, I think most of them have yellow parts, not blue as I thought. But the photo shows one with a blue head. Sight is a problem. I can't get close to them with my reading glasses and they're too small for my distance glasses.

And then I saw a red-breasted bird.

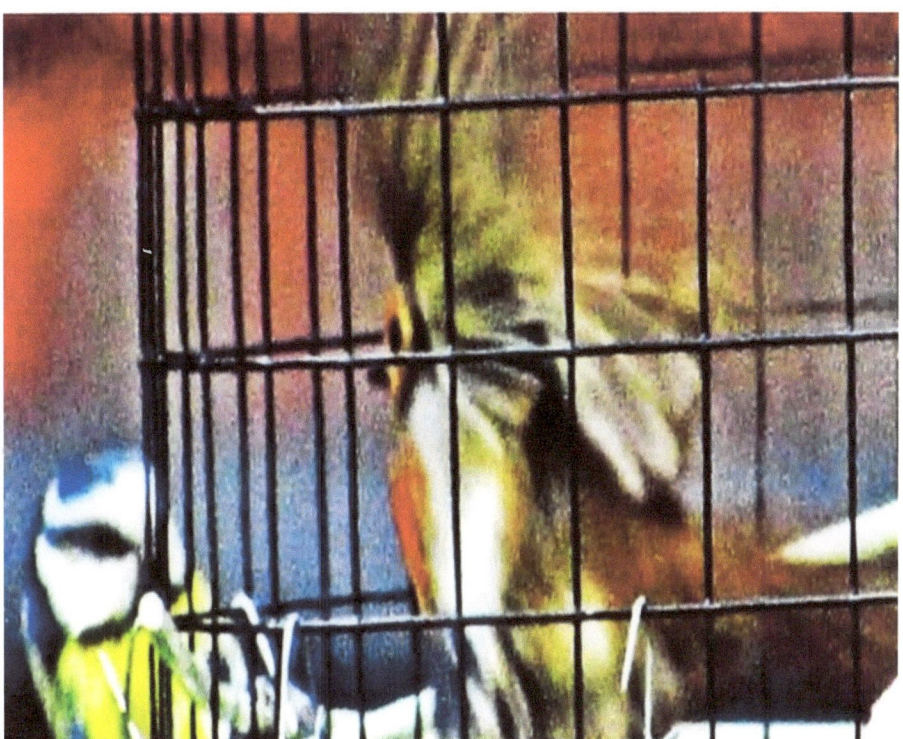

A neighbour told me it was a robin, but I couldn't tell the difference at first. The tits would go straight to the feeder to take the food, while the robins would perch on any spot with a good view nearby and look at the area for a long time before going to the bottom plate to choose the tits spilled fooled they liked.

This went on for a long time. Then, a few months later, things had partly reversed or they mimicked each other. I saw tits going to the plate to choose their food, and a few times I saw a robin in a cage by the garden fence, hanging from the net of the feeder without any elegance. I thought that robins were a bit clumsy, and with the tits spilling seeds on the plates, there was no need for them going to the feeders' net to imitate the tits.

The photo page 23 shows a robin fighting or trying to frighten a bird with a blue head. In the photo the robin's head is covered with standing feathers. Was the robin fearful or angry?

The Winter Palace was empty and needed a companion. I moved the new cage feeder close to this festival of colour and hung the new bird cage from the end of the long stick (in the photo is a Long John, my mistake, always doings changes).

I knew that the bright, unusual colours of the Winter Palace, as I knew them from the tropics, might frighten the birds, but the proximity of the food would encourage them to visit the palace.

This did not happen, and I gave up as you learn ahead.

I liked the new arrangement, but every time I went to the shed to get the trike to go for tennis, I had to fight the long, awkward roll of chicken wire that was still there. I had no problem with that. The only problem was that I didn't have room for it.

I made another cage feeder, then another and another, seven in all. The birds were happy, the squirrels not so much, but the cats were.

I like cats. They're independent.

I like them all: small, big, fast, very big, even the old ones, the sabre-toothed cats.

Some cats live far away, which is good because they can roar and we know they are far away.

Cats are everywhere: in comics, cartoons and every other genre.

Some small ones come close and their prrr ask for our attention, which usually demands too much of us unless we understand them, which is not my forte. Somehow, in my case, I think they know me better than I know them.

These little visitors made me sad. One of them had done something wrong and I had to change my attitude because I had become the protector of the birds and squirrels. I control their numbers with my feeders as cheaply as I can, but I would never kill them.

A cat did. It killed the adult squirrel and destroyed the blackbird nest, probably killing the chick. The central bush in the prior photo, where the blackbird couple's nest was, which had been a permanent airport for birds landing, mainly from the neighbour's large building yard or elsewhere, became completely silent and static.

Even now, months after the massacre, only one robin visits the bush before taking a dip in the swimming pool on the lower central wall on the left, a kind of island that divides the garden.

Mr Carlton, a neighbour, had placed two large empty Icelandic chicken packs with water near the central bush. You can see it in the photo and the robin on the front cover of this booklet is bathing in one of them.

The bush itself did not like what was happening. Half the bush dried up and was cut down by the council gardeners.

The robin is still there, keeping watch on the wall. He does this before taking a long bath.

Note: the photo above is my final photograph for this booklet, another bird, not a robin, perches on the remains of the dead half of the central bush. Is it a sparrow? I really did not find references for it.

I hope they don't nest in that middle bush. It brings back bad memories. These days the cats are a bit scared of me because I frown, make scary noises and they go away.

However, there is one ginger cat, I don't know if he's half domesticated or a stray, who likes to wander around when he doesn't see me. The other five are very cautious, probably preferring a life inside the house to getting into trouble with a human.

I know there are some sparrows here, but I think they are only one colour. I remember them from when I was a child in Lisbon, but that was a long time ago.

I was also lucky enough to see two woodpeckers! I was right, because I saw them pecking at one of the trees. But they didn't stay long, probably because the tree was not right or there were too many people around.

Alas, I also found a medium-sized bird in one of the feeders by the neighbour's fence. I saw it again in the same place the next day. Unfortunately, it was dead.

I can't say for sure whether it died of exhaustion from trying to find food on the spot or from frustration at not being able to get into its cage.

After checking my intelligent sources, I identified it as a starling. The bird was beautiful. It had many striped colours, much more subtle than I had expected. Colours you can see up close, though not visible because they're always far away.

I had to adjust my feelings.

I had to reread my favourite poem about birds, especially starlings.

Elizabeth from Greenwich corrected it by adding a special touch. I've never known her personally. We communicated online in a group where everyone talked about how wonderful it was to be able to write about anything in complete freedom, without being corrected or paying anything, and at that time nobody used photos. That freedom didn't last long.

Her son had an accident and I dedicated other poems to him. I sent her the poem and she improved it.

I dedicated this poem to Mary Ann, a friend from Seattle, who corrected my little book of poems in English.

Hi Mary Ann

How is our forest today?
The wind through the leaves
A moment of silence
A shuffle somewhere
A scuffle nearby
No! We relax.
Perhaps a bird
Splashing the wings in a pothole
Sometimes stopping all movements
Or caught up in a tic, head up, then
Head leaning to the right, to the left
Ridiculous in only one eye stare
As a bird can be.
Relaxed again, we have
Only another second, less or more
And in the air
Against the bright side of some clouds
Thousands of starlings fluxing
Correcting the alphabet
Time over time, again and again
Without possible count
Going back and forward
Opening and closing the dictionary
In constant brushed circles
Unsuccessful each time
Unsatisfied with the calligraphy.
Thank God! Wonderful!
For our delight!

An army of parakeets once visited us. More than the ones in the photo.

Once! Most of them perched on the roof while a few bravely come down to explore the cages. I am sure some of them had seen the little birds eating there before. Two of them even tested a cage by hanging from its side.

The cage swung and stayed tilted. The feeder inside was free and stayed upright, coming very close to the net where they were. The clever nerd used its beak to pull the feeder close to the cage net, allowing the other parrot to pick up the seeds. Later, the adaptable one grabbed one of the feeder's metal rings with his claws and was able to feed himself.

It was the first time a parakeet had tasted the food. I thought the whole school would invade the garden and take over. But that didn't happen, it wasn't a school, I believe, it was a pandemonium.

I had to do something. I waited a few weeks to see what would happen. A lot of things happened, a lot of things developed, and after that fortnight I had three problems to deal with.

First of all, three troubles are better than an infinite number of other troubles, because the problems with these three never seemed to end. They were the squirrels, the parakeets and the pigeons.

I used to feed the squirrels separately from the cages.

This did not work as I expected. They thanked me like a bad lover and always ran to the next food source, regardless of the obstacle in front of them.

Squirrels have no clear territory to defend with their eyes and teeth to keep out rivals.

They go everywhere. They see where the food is, not because the food is there, but because they see other squirrels getting fatter.

Many birds can be seen going in and out of the cages and perching everywhere. Pigeons rest on the pipes and on the verandas and facades of nearby buildings. Squirrels also use the pipes, clearly wanting to be part of the daily party of garden enjoyment. The photo shows the pipes.

Other squirrels, the new masters of the block, come down from the tallest trees around the railway behind our building to bully our little ones - the twins.

The squirrel in the photo, Popcorn, is sitting peacefully at the bottom of their Long John, munching on a peanut. The metal plate had to be changed. Revising the book, I'm sad, he has disappeared. The story is the same.

I ignore those who come from outside, but I must tell you about Popcorn and his brother.

They are twin brothers. They were born on our beautiful deciduous trees, photo next page. The colour of the leaves heralds a new winter.

As babies, coming down the tree, they played with each other all the time. When they were a bit older, they played alone with the little branches that fell from the trees to the ground or bits of litter.

Now that they're little adults, they go their separate ways and never come together to eat.

But there was one special exception this winter, which I'll tell you about later.

The twins have got used to me since they came down from the trees. One of them even came up to my hand to get some peanuts, but in his own way he nibbled at one of my fingers. It wasn't a big bite, just a little touch, and he did that to check things out. I decided that day to be African and let the wild animals be wild. They know me, I know them, but that's it. Each enjoys their independent side of life.

We then had two types of squirrel groups: one was really strong and survivalist and the other was just learning the few boundaries I had set for all the birds and squirrels.

Imitation is a quality that worries me a little. Some people are lucky enough to be themselves, to learn from others and to be independent. The reality for me is that most people prefer the easy way out, and that has many facets.

My readings have shown that conformity is one of the most important human behaviours, and imitation is part of it.

I was careful and safe, and I'm sure you will be too.

I saw that the cages were damaged, so I waited patiently for hours to catch the culprits. The master squirrels were just doing what they thought was natural or what they knew best, but the young twins saw them causing trouble. Not good!

Imitation, right, that was the point. I had to change my approach, and fast.

I had to find a way to keep the squirrels away from the birds' cages and feeders. I had to be firm, and when our local squirrels tried to copy the foreigners, I had to stop them.

Birds and squirrels school each other: Phillip, think!

The twins may have backed up trying to damage the cages in front of me.

I know they are naughty toddlers and I had to deal with the situation. Leisure or not, I knew I was in charge.

But that wasn't enough.

I started to notice a few other things that needed attention, and once again... things got a bit confusing.

I'll talk about the new cages later, but in the meantime, I noticed that the pigeons were perching on the branches I'd placed around the bottom of the cages. Then I saw them stick their little heads up to their shoulders in the larger holes in the netting I did so they could easily reach the food on the plates inside the cages. I put these extra plates on the top of fixed ones for easy cleaning and also catch the spilling.

I felt it was a competition, my artificiality against nature.

Nature never ceases to surprise us. The pigeons loved to eat the food that fell from the feeders onto the plates below.

The robins loved to eat the food that spilled from the feeders onto the plates below. One little tit had a special talent. Unlike the others, he liked to stay at the feeder for a long time, deliberately dropping seeds for the robins.

The other tits came and went quickly, but this one stayed in the cage. Isn't it interesting how birds can be like us? Some have their own personality and don't care what others think of them.

The parakeets also found these larger holes and two of them copied the pigeons by approaching the cage. After a while one of them even got into the cage through a two-inch hole, but he couldn't get out easily, so I got the cage and I carefully removed the parakeet and I must say that this little green bird was furious!

His beak was so determined to get at my fingers that I had to be very careful.

I didn't see them again for a while. I know

33

for a fact that parakeets really do tell each other everything that happens.

The little one, who was a prisoner for five minutes, told them that I kept his frustrated beak away from my fingers.

They stopped coming and not everything I write is the truth, be aware of my irony, after all I have had a lot, I know that, but they were feelings, they are not right or wrong only that they needed some soothing time at the right time.

We had a couple of parakeets in the garden this winter and one of them went into the squirrels' Long John a couple of times (prior photo). No problem, I had anticipated that, but not the timings. They do not stay if they see the squirrels.

I think it was only one that went into the cage. The other, which is not in the photo, stayed outside in obvious frustration, first looking at its mate and then, as with the smaller single feeder cages, trying unsuccessfully to tilt the cage to reach one of the two feeders.

The pair have returned, but not for the Long John. I'm not sure if they are the same birds. It's clear that the birds prefer to tilt the smaller cages to get to the feeder inside than to visit the inside of the Long Johns.

I can see why, because the Long Johns, which are longer cages, are difficult to tilt. Anyway, I don't mind the few parakeets that visit us, it's always a pleasant surprise to see them, I think I'm in Chitado, Cunene, close to Namibia, where I've seen thousands of them, a real pandemonium, but in different colours and sizes.

Kept out of the cage's insides, awkward, they snack more than they eat, and there's plenty of food for any bird smart enough to know what it wants. Once again, it's a pleasure to see them.

The original cage feeders have been replaced with new ones. These new feeders have been modified to prevent pigeons and squirrels from damaging them.

To achieve this, the two-inch holes in the new cylinders, photo, are now at least ten centimetres above the bottom of the cage. No problem for the paraquets.

The behaviour of the tits is a little surprising. Most of them fly straight to the feeder without even touching the net and then fly back the same way. It takes them a split second to leave the feeder. It's amazing how they do it.

Some tits are just patient, as if they're waiting for the right moment, like robins do. It's as if they're playing tit for tat, tit imitating robin, and then tat, robin imitating tit.

I never expected that. I'm not an expert in birds, so I'm not sure if boffins study their appearance or their behaviour.

I think it's something called ethology, but I'm not sure. I don't know if the name applies to birds.

My new job is to feed them, which is really nice, and I also have to clean and wash the cages, which is also a nice chore. It's a lot more than I expected, but I'm enjoying it.

The new parakeet and pigeon proof cage pictured below is interesting. It's much wider, so it's much harder to tilt, and if you do, the feeder never gets close enough to the net.

At first it was a great success, but I have to say it's been a bit difficult lately. I'm not a tree expert, so I have no idea what's happening to our trees and shrubs as the seasons change. I don't even know what they're doing in terms of releasing aromas, perfumes, flavours or even toxic substances.

I've placed the larger cage under a lovely evergreen tree, I think it's a spruce, but I haven't seen many birds feeding in it lately as I used to. Only when it's been raining, I have seen birds feeding there. Or the birds change their preferences, some cages today, others tomorrow, like in a commando operation, the way to the target is different from the way back, all for safety reasons.

Another person complained that the birds had disappeared from her garden, also with a lot of feeders, so I'm more relaxed about it.

When I replaced the first few cages with new ones, I kept the ones with very large holes for another time.

I continued to feed my little squirrels. They would run around and look at me as if to say, "Thanks for the food, but we'd rather have something else." So, I gave them some of the food that the birds had rejected. I even tried some breakfast cereal that I couldn't eat, but that didn't work either. They were very patient and kept coming closer and closer to me in increasing numbers like saying, "Decide, we want proper food!"

My mind was on them.

I knew I had to do something. I saw the twins running, jumping, checking and even waiting for the squirrel chiefs to eat first when they visited the garden, or being chased away if they were there for lunch before the chiefs arrived.

Long Johns

I needed help to find more motivation and new solutions.

I relaxed, I played tennis for a few days and enjoyed long talks with my girlfriend.

I came up with the Long Johns.

I made two.

I bought plates or saucers for all the cages I already had, and the same for the new ones I wanted to make.

A full set or pair is quite expensive, so imagine seven sets! I bought fourteen saucers, the new ones being bigger than the old ones I'd already bought. I also discovered that the larger holes I had made in the first cages needed to be corrected, as some of them were too close to the bottom.

The first Long John was built with the first used cages. I put the two rejected cages together, one on top of the other, while

being careful where the holes were.

I didn't think it through and put saucers on both sides.

The second was made with the last remnants of virgin netting, also with the plates embroidered on both sides. The prior photo shows the Long John of the Squirrels with all the transformations I have discovered so far.

I had a deception with the plates, mainly because the squirrels showed no interest, they did not use the Long Johns to feed.

I had not planned it well.

After a few thoughts about the little guys, I finally decided to take the saucer from the top of the new cage and replace the one at the bottom with a smaller one, so not really covering the bottom.

I made it the squirrel feeder. Finally, after what seemed like months of work, I had something that worked.

I left the original holes, one inch in size, so not too many birds would get through. Sorry, time goes by and a few tits have learned to use the free top to get down to the feeders. Only a few, interesting.

I recently saw two parakeets land on it for the first time on their Long John, which was a very special moment for me. We'll see what happens next.

The feeder is very long and doesn't come close to the net, so the parakeets can't nibble at the seeds by tilting the cage, but the cage has big entrances on the top for them to get in and out.

It hasn't happened yet. I'm not sure they'll use them, we'll see. It's clear that they prefer the old small cages that they can tilt.

The new Long John feeder for squirrels has now two feeders, one for seeds and the other, underneath, for peanuts.

I have to say that the little four-legged guys are lucky! The Long John squirrel cage has now six half-brooms, so the little guys can sit down, chew and eat the peanuts or seeds relaxed. Interestingly, they prefer the bottom plate.

They will only stay if they feel safe. If not, they run up the tree or down to the ground. Both sides are open.

Back to the squirrels and Long-John's squirrel cage (photo page 38). The feeder has only two holes on the bottom, which is what I wanted because it limits the speed at which the squirrels can eat the peanuts. At the moment, it lasts a week.

With these restrictions, I hope the other neighbour's wild squirrels won't visit us anymore. It is my wish, I must say, it saves money as well, and that's my ultimate compromise and goal.

I have written before about exceptions:

I once saw the young adult twins meet again as they were toddlers, which was a real surprise. The bigger one led the smaller one to the squirrel cage and they ate the food at the same time, an even bigger surprise. I'm not sure if it was teaching, compassion, brotherhood or something else, but it was heartwarming to see.

One twin is much bigger than the other. It's survival of the fittest. The smaller one has taken up residence in the spruce above the larger cage. That may be why the birds aren't feeding in that cage. I'm not sure why, though. I checked the cage today and saw some birds there. Again, I am not sure.

The sibling rendezvous didn't happen again, so I think the bigger one, Mr Popcorn, was just showing the twin, who I've now named Mr Squirrel, how to get food when the Long John is empty of the live teeth, legs and arms of other county squirrels.

I'm sure it was just a special moment, a family thing.

Other Observations

The weather plays a big part in a garden full of trees and small creatures. We had a big storm and some of the saucers flew out of their cages. Every problem has a solution.

I bought some little bungee cords and froze the saucers to the cages, so they no longer will fly.

We had another storm with high winds, but luckily nothing happened. The inner plates on the top and on the bottom saucers, which catch the spillage from the feeders, are inverted and this cancel each other out or, aerodynamically, the effect of the wind on them.

The bungee cords were really effective, they kept everything in place even when the wind reached 50 miles per hour.

I don't really know that much about birds and squirrels, but I'm happy to share what I do know. What I wanted was separate them.

Like I said, I just want to make sure the little birds are fed, safe and happy. But I have to say that the bigger birds like the pigeons, parakeets and magpies have taught me a thing or two.

I was really surprised by the pigeon-gang - those pigeons we all see on the streets. They are fast and always in groups, and I think the size of the groups depends on the amount of food available.

It's great to see them flying in pairs or small groups, and the smaller pigeons always outperform the larger wood pigeons (photo). It's a real treat to see the two species here, and I think it's even better that they're both here. It's not really a competition though.

It's funny how the wood pigeon Mr Snow always seems to be on the losing side. I had to stop feeding him privately with peanuts because the gang learned my calls and came faster than he did. I had the idea of feeding a lone friend instead of the gang, but it didn't quite work out as planned. Mr Snow was not a fighter, he would give up immediately when the gang would get close.

He was also very much like me, cautious and shy. The idea of feeding a lonely friend instead of the gang, which was the pattern of my life, didn't work out as planned.

But the street pigeons, even if it's just one, can hold their own against the magpies (photos below). The black and white birds scurry away when the pigeons harass them, but the magpies wait patiently for one of them to get tired, sick and die so they can take their revenge.

Robins and tits, parakeets and magpies, pigeons, even crows - I recently saw a gull in a chimney on our roof, it did not last - and other birds are learning from each other or adapting to circumstances.

Finally, it's almost spring and the tits are changing their preferences.

    They used to feed in the cages in the most sheltered parts of the garden, but lately they've been feeding near the bushes where they nest. Look at the picture next page, the summer leaves on the bush are not yet in place, but the chickadees (USA name) have already taken over.

    The tall bush is where the tits like to nest and the Long John (for birds) that serves them is visible. I'm not sure if they'll nest there this year as the council have cut the bush in half and it's much smaller now so it's not as protective.

    Today I saw a parakeet trying to get food from a normal cage. It came alone and didn't succeed because it needs a partner to add weight to tilt the cage and bring the feeder close to their feet and beak.

Another image that still sticks in my mind is of a pigeon that didn't know what peanuts were. It took him a while to pick one up

from the ground and then more.

But immediately two other pigeons came down from the neighbour's roof and swooped down near him, not once but twice, forcing him to go with them and ignore the peanuts.

To me, it was the parents and a small child being told not to trust food given by humans.

I was stunned.

That's how it is in the wild, and it's all part of the ongoing cycle of nature. The two photos show an interaction between them.

I've got the video, but it's clear that the magpies are giving up food for the pigeons. In the second photo you can see the magpie flying away from the food ball. In another photo, the parakeets on the cage nets looking for a snack do not like the pigeons coming closer. The photos, page 46, show the parakeet's aggressiveness.

As I look back on my last summer, which felt like one long non-stop memory, I would like to share a few thoughts with you.

The bushes and trees change during the autumn and winter, and some even flower in winter, which the tits love.

They also love a dense tree that has lost its leaves. It has many fine branches and twigs that are too close together for cats and squirrels to get into.

Birds need water. It's a good idea to put a bowl of water around the cages. I had a couple of porcelain ones, but they all broke when the freezing cold expanded the water. It was especially sad because the Winter Palace was beautifully decorated with one, but now it's gone. I put trays on the top of some bird cages, but the wind made them fall over, so now I put a stone inside each one.

I feed birds and squirrels.

I buy whatever is cheaper, so I am not sure if I am doing the right thing.

I really have tried different options such as dry worms, peanut kernels, peanuts (not good for chicks, avoid them in the first part of their life), a mix of seeds and kernels and sunflower seeds.

Because of the price (more expensive in winter) I prefer to buy sunflower seeds for the birds and peanuts for the squirrels.

I have been doing this for a while now, through summer, autumn and winter, and I am getting ready for spring.

We had lots of birds in the summer, but not anymore. The birds we have now are bigger, probably adults. I don't know what happened to the little tits, unless some have grown up. I have a prior observation about this, for me a phenomenon.

There are a lot more robins than there used to be, five or six times more, but it is clear that they are very territorial, as are the cages. I have seen some in pairs recently.

We have had problems with people. Some of the neighbours are feeding pigeons... and, sadly, rats. It's quieter now, but the danger is still there.

Sunshine Invites Birds

The photo below shows two parakeets and two tits in two

cages under the same tree (winter time).

One parakeet is ready to leave while the other parakeet is surprised by its companion because it cannot reach the feeder on its own. They need to be together to do it. One tit is drinking water while the other tit is at the bottom of the cage, doing what robins usually do: perching on something, looking around and picking up the seeds at the bottom because it feels safe.

The photo below is another bird that never goes into the cages but loves the sunshine. The big eye on its back is not the bird's eye. It is too big to be a sparrow, but you never know. I did not find it in the photos I looked.

Another February surprise: after months of no contact with the bird cages, I saw, it seemed, a little sparrow entering into one today. Imitation again? The last bird photo, taken during the winter, is about cold.

A summary about cage feeders

The Long Johns for the squirrels, which are open at the top, need more sticks than the others (I use six in total, crossed). There is a picture in the book showing the six sticks. Now let's talk about protecting your bird feeders from squirrels, pigeons and parakeets. You will probably need to build a cage for the squirrels to stop them damaging the bird cages. Parakeets will sometimes use the Long John, but if you build a normal cage with a small diameter, they will learn to tilt it to eat.

For the birds:

Use chicken wire with 1-inch holes.

I bought 20 metres on eBay, but the price and length of the roll will vary. The width of the net should be the same as the height of the outer cage.

The diameter of the normal cage should be about 46-47cm to protect this one feeder cage from pigeons and parakeets.

The bottom and top have vase plates, about 50cm outside diameter (also available on eBay).

I find the black ones look best. I use black spray paint for the wire as it is a neutral colour and makes the cage almost invisible, making it easier to see and photograph the birds. Paint

the net tangentially to save paint.

Use broom handles, old or new (you can find these on eBay) and paint them black. Tighten one side at the top and attach the hook in the middle to hold the feeder. Then run a cable/wire from the two outer ends of the top and hook it somewhere in the middle to a chain on a tree branch so that the cage hangs no more than two metres off the ground (from the top of the cage, for maintenance). I use metal chains because parakeets and squirrels are big gnawers.

Use two widths of chicken wire for the Long Johns for the squirrels. Cut them evenly and the diameter can be a little smaller than 46-47cm. Join them together on top of each other. I use two bird feeders in my Long John squirrel feeder. I put birdseed on the top and peanuts on the bottom.

I put a vase saucer at the bottom of the Long John. This saucer is slightly smaller than the diameter of the cage. I attached it to the sides of the cage with fine florist's wire, but make sure the small squirrels can still get through the gap between the tray or plate and the net. This allows them to escape from other squirrels and cats.

About holes. The most important thing is the size of the holes in the mesh. Small tits can use one-inch holes to get through the cage net. Larger birds, such as great tits and adult robins, need at least two-inch holes to get through. I have seen small squirrels get through these holes, so provide a separate cage feeder for them. Have a look at the photos in the book.

I have a Long John with 2"x3" holes (it was for the parakeets, so far, they did not use it), but make sure the holes aren't too close to the bottom of the cage. If you only have one feeder, do not do this. It is better to have a second cage for this option not including the cage for the squirrels. You can make larger holes in the middle and at the top of the cage.

Look at the different bird feeders in the photos. Some were cheap and some more expensive.

Look at the two types of birdseed I use. It is an experience. I have a feeling they rejected the last batch of black seed (sunflower) I bought, but I don't know why. Probably ice or wet, I don't know. Now they have two options. Again, most have left the garden, as another friend told me, so it is not just here.

The Long John at the previous page has the most expensive feeder I have ever bought. It is long and has four holes with small perches in each.

I also had to solve the mystery of the Winter Palace. I gave up to put seeds inside. I took the bottom lid and all the food inside. I washed the inside of the palace thoroughly and left the bottom of the palace completely open. It is now open and free. I have seen many tits going in and out as they seem to play.

Since then, they sometimes use it as a safe place to fly to the cages and back, more like a stopover before flying to a bush or tree.

There are many details that are not mentioned here, but you can learn them by watching and getting experience.

*

My experience cost a lot of money, mainly because I was trying to build the best cage, so I built eight to get there. The first one was the most artistic, an endless bag with no bottom, but also because I didn't know what I was doing. My only aim was to keep the birds safe and well fed according to their size.

The End

Zebras Also Have a Garden of Flowers

2025-2026

After finishing the book some time ago, I felt a sense of accomplishment. Since then, I have enjoyed feeding and watching the birds at the eight bird feeders in the garden. Sadly, most of the birds were wiped out by an illness — probably bird flu. It was sad to see all my little friends disappear one by one. The six visiting squirrels disappeared too. Only the two little brothers who were born in one of the trees pictured in the following pages remained in the garden. One developed well, while the other stayed small. At one point, almost against their nature and instincts, I saw the big brother protect the little one a few times and teach him how to use the Long John feeders.

By summer 2025, hardly any birds remained. Their secluded garden had been their winter home, almost like a protected reserve, but when summer arrived, they probably flew to greener pastures, possibly to local parks with lots of trees.

The big brother squirrel, who was familiar with me, disappeared, as did the little squirrel that lived in one of the garden trees. However, he frequently returns to raid the Long John squirrel feeder. He never managed to master the peanut feeder below, whereas his brother used to empty it every two or three days.

The new summer brought new pigeons, but no magpies. The pigeons were raised on our neighbour's roof and I interacted with them a few times when they were very young. Their parents even flew at me like fighter planes in a raid when I offered food to the fledglings. One stubborn young pigeon, probably hungry, stayed behind and ignored its parents. After a few raids, it finally left the peanuts on the ground.

Once they had become independent, they moved to the surrounding roofs of our large garden. When the sister of our building coordinator gave me some bird feeders, I used the heaviest one to create a feeder for the pigeons, which I hung two metres above the grass. They have to establish a pecking order, which reduces the number of pigeons coming to the garden.

From summer 2025 onwards, birds of different species stopped competing with each other physically. Recently, a few parakeets have started visiting the garden again and at least one of them regularly feeds from the second Long John feeder. He doesn't like going inside the first Long John feeder, which has no top, although one photo shows him doing so.

In winter, tits remain the most common birds in the area. The six robins that I used to see defending their territories have disappeared. I recently saw one, but I'm unsure of its territory.

The photos show birds and squirrels in summer and winter, as well as the pigeon feeder that was once visited by a parakeet. It snowed in January 2026.

www.ingramcontent.com/pod-product-compliance
Lightning Source LLC
LaVergne TN
LVHW072113070426
835510LV00002B/33